Sound and Light

Karen Bryant-Mole

RIGBY
INTERACTIVE
LIBRARY

This edition © 1997 Rigby Education
Published by Rigby Interactive Library,
an imprint of Rigby Education,
division of Reed Elsevier, Inc.
Chicago, Illinois

Customer Service 888-454-2279

Visit our website at www.heinemannlibrary.com

© BryantMole Books 1998

Printed and bound in Hong Kong
Cover designed by Lisa Buckley
Interior designed by Jean Wheeler
Commissioned photography by Sharon Hoogstraten and Zul Mukhida
Consultant: Hazel Grice

06 05 04 03 02
10 9 8 7 6 5 4

Library of Congress Cataloging-in-Publication Data
Bryant-Mole, Karen.
        Sound and Light / by Karen Bryant-Mole.
            p.   cm. -- (Science all around me)
        Includes bibliographical references and index.
        Summary: Explains the basic principles of sound and light through looking at everyday experiences and direct observation.
        ISBN 1-57572-111-2 (lib. bdg.)   ISBN 1-4034-0055-5 (pbk. bdg.)
        1. Sound—Juvenile literature. 2. Light—Juvenile literature. [1. Sound. 2. Light] I. Title. II. Series
QC225.5.B79   1996
534—dc20   96-22976
                                                                                                    CIP
                                                                                                    AC

Acknowledgments
The Publishers would like to thank the following for permission to reproduce photographs: Chapel Studios pp.10, 14;
Eye Ubiquitous pp. 4, 20; Positive Images p. 22; Tony Stone Images p.6 (Nicole Katano), p. 8 (Mark Wagner), p. 12 (Tim Davis); Zefa pp. 16, 18.

Every effort has been made to contact copyright holders of any material reproduced in this book.
Any omissions will be rectified in subsequent printings if notice is given to the Publisher.

Words that appear in the text in **bold** can be found in the glossary.

Contents

What Is Sound?

A sound is made when something vibrates, or wobbles, very quickly.

The sound made by these musical instruments **travels** to the ears of the people all around them.

Sounds make **liquid** in your ears vibrate. Your brain understands these vibrations as sounds.

? *What are some sounds you hear every day?*

See for Yourself . . .

Sometimes you can see objects vibrating as they make sounds.

Put half of a plastic ruler under a book. Hold down the book and the ruler with one hand.

With the other hand, bend the other end of the ruler downward. When you let go, the ruler will vibrate and make a sound.

High and Low

Some objects vibrate quickly.
Other objects vibrate slowly.

The faster the vibration,
the higher the sound.
The slower the vibration,
the lower the sound.

When this violin makes
high sounds, its strings
vibrate quickly.

? *What are some
things that make a
low sound?*

See for Yourself . . .

Stretch a rubber band around an open empty box. Pluck the rubber band and watch it vibrate.

Collect some rubber bands of different lengths. Put these on your box.

The tighter the rubber band, the higher the sound it makes.

Loud and Soft

Some sounds are soft.
Others are loud.

Leaves brushing together on the
branches of trees make a soft sound.

This plane makes a very loud sound
as it takes off.

? *Can you think
of anything else
that makes a
loud sound?*

See for Yourself . . .

Whispers are very soft noises. They are sometimes difficult to hear.

Yasmin and her friends are sitting in a circle. Yasmin whispers a **sentence** to Kitty. Kitty whispers what she thinks she hears to Maya, and so on.

By the time it gets back to Yasmin, the sentence might be very different!

Sound Makers

Sounds can be made by many different objects.

Look at this picture.

The tape recorder can play story tapes. The alarm clock can ring. The guitar can be used to make music.

? *What objects around your house make a sound?*

See for Yourself . . .

Collect some objects that make a sound.

Listen to each sound and decide whether the sound is high or low, loud or soft.

Next, try to think of words, such as *buzz, ding,* or *hoot,* that describe the sound each object makes.

People and Animals

People and animals make sounds, too.

People can laugh and cry. We put sounds together in different ways to make words.

This dog can bark and yelp.

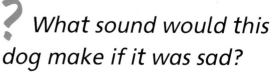 *What sound would this dog make if it was sad?*

See for Yourself . . .

We make sounds when special flaps of skin in our throats vibrate.

Place your hand across the front of your throat.

Put your lips together and make a low, humming sound. Can you feel the vibrations through your fingers?

Traveling Sound

Every quarter of an hour, large bells inside this clock tower ring. People living near the clock hear a very loud sound.

People living many streets away can hear the clock, too. But the sound they hear is much softer.

(i) *The further you are from the source of a sound, the quieter it seems.*

See for Yourself . . .

Find a small clock that ticks. Put it to your ear. How loud is the ticking?

Put the clock down on a table. How loud is the ticking sound now?

Now walk away from the clock. How well can you hear the ticking? Why?

What Is Light?

Light is a form of **energy**.

This bulb lights up when electricity flows through a thin wire inside it. The wire heats up and makes a white light.

Objects that give out their own light are called *luminous*.

(i) *Televisions and computer screens are luminous, too.*

See for Yourself . . .

Shiny objects sometimes look luminous.
This is because light from something else
is bouncing off them.

Put some objects
on a table. Ask a
friend to help you
decide which of
the objects are
luminous.

How many did
you find?

Sunlight

? *Can you see the rays of sunlight streaming through these trees?*

Sunlight is a very important source of light.

Sunlight helps us to see. Plants need sunlight to grow. All the food that we eat comes from plants or from animals that eat plants.

18

See for Yourself . . .

How is making a cheese sandwich related to sunlight? To find out, take one slice of the food that is made of wheat, which needs sunlight to grow. Next, put on the food that is made from milk, which comes from cows, who eat grass, which needs sunlight to grow. Top that with another slice of the food made from wheat. Enjoy!

Darkness

Where there is no light, there is darkness. It is impossible to see anything in complete darkness.

This photograph was taken at night. Although it looks quite dark, it is not completely dark.

Moonlight and the lights in our homes and streets help us to see at night.

Earth spins around the sun. This gives us day and night.

20

See for Yourself . . .

Find out how to make day turn into night. Use a flashlight for the sun and a ball for Earth. Put a sticker on the ball to mark a place on Earth.

Shine the light at the sticker. Ask a friend to slowly spin the ball.

What happens to the sticker? It moves from "day" to "night."

Shadows

Some materials, such as air and glass, let light pass right through them.

Many objects do not let light pass through them. Instead, a *shadow,* or an area of darkness, is made behind them.

The wood, metal, and string in this hammock do not let light through. But the air between them does.

? *What do you think made the other shadows in this picture?*

See for Yourself . . .

Shine a beam of light from the flashlight onto a white wall.

Put your hands between the light and the wall. Move your hands to make funny shapes. What happens? Why?

Your hands make shadows because light cannot pass through them.

Glossary

Index

Further Readings

Cooper, Jason. *Sound.* Rourke Corporation, 1992.

Gibson, Gary. *Hearing Sounds.* Copper Beech Books, 1994.

Verdet, Jean-Pierre. *Light.* Scholastic, 1994.

Davies, Kay. *Light.* Steck-Vaughn Company, 1992.

Answers

p. 4, alarm clock, family members talking, school bell; p. 6, hum of refridgerator, cat purring; p. 12, whimper; p. 22, the tree.